ORCA
Think

Question, connect and take action to become better citizens
with a brighter future. Now that's smart thinking!

GOOD FOOD, BAD WASTE

Let's Eat for the Planet

Erin Silver

illustrated by Suharu Ogawa

ORCA BOOK PUBLISHERS

Published in Canada and the United States in 2023 by Orca Book Publishers.
orcabook.com

Library and Archives Canada Cataloguing in Publication
Title: Good food, bad waste : let's eat for the planet / Erin Silver ; illustrated by Suharu Ogawa.
Names: Silver, Erin, 1980- author. | Ogawa, Suharu, 1979- illustrator.
Series: Orca think ; 9.
Description: Series statement: Orca think ; 9 | Includes bibliographical references and index.
Identifiers: Canadiana (print) 20220250189 | Canadiana (ebook) 20220250197 |
ISBN 9781459830912 (hardcover) | ISBN 9781459830929 (PDF) | ISBN 9781459830936 (EPUB)
Subjects: LCSH: Food waste—Juvenile literature. | LCSH: Food waste—Environmental aspects—Juvenile literature. | LCSH: Food waste—Prevention—Juvenile literature.
Classification: LCC HD9000.5 .S49 2023 | DDC j363.72/88—dc23

Library of Congress Control Number: 2022938873

Summary: Part of the nonfiction Orca Think series for middle-grade readers, this illustrated book examines the problem of food waste around the world, its consequences for the environment and practical things young readers can do to curb food waste.

Orca Book Publishers is committed to reducing the consumption of nonrenewable resources in the production of our books. We make every effort to use materials that support a sustainable future.

Orca Book Publishers gratefully acknowledges the support for its publishing programs provided by the following agencies: the Government of Canada, the Canada Council for the Arts and the Province of British Columbia through the BC Arts Council and the Book Publishing Tax Credit.

Cover and interior artwork by Suharu Ogawa
Design by Dahlia Yuen
Edited by Kirstie Hudson

Printed and bound in South Korea.

26 25 24 23 • 1 2 3 4

This book is dedicated to my mom,
who composted before it was cool and always
turns leftovers into tasty new meals.

Contents

Introduction

The idea for this book came from my fridge. Well, from all the food in my fridge. One day after buying groceries, I opened the fridge door and realized I'd bought more milk, meat, fruits and vegetables than my family could eat in the week. I hadn't stuck to my shopping list. I hadn't made a meal plan. Now I was faced with a problem: how was my family going to finish what we had?

While some families don't have enough to eat, others have plenty, and food rots in the fridge or gets thrown out. In fact, **food waste** is a major problem all over the world. Every day, in grocery stores, restaurants, our homes and even school cafeterias, good food is tossed in the trash. And not just a few leftover peas from your dinner plate or the crusts from your sandwich at lunch. We're talking about massive amounts of usable food, in countries around the globe. According to a 2021 **United Nations (UN)** study of global food waste, almost a billion tons (900 million metric tons) of food get thrown away each year. That's enough to feed three billion people, in a time when at least 900 million suffer from hunger.

Most of this wasted food ends up rotting in *landfills*. And that's a huge problem. The UN report also found that up to 10 percent of global ***greenhouse gas emissions*** are caused by wasted food. This means that all the food we don't eat contributes to global warming. What's the connection? Keep flipping the pages to find out.

The good news is that many countries have promised to cut food waste in half by 2030. It's a big undertaking. But if we all work together, we can meet this goal and make sure hungry people have access to food. And by reducing food waste, we'll be fighting the climate crisis at the same time. With some simple, easy tips, you can cut food waste starting today. *Good Food, Bad Waste* will teach you how—and give you lots of information to chew on!

One
Full Fridges and Family-Sized Foods

Did your parents ever tell you not to waste food because people in other countries are starving? Well, people in your own class could be hungry too. **Food insecurity** affects approximately 13 million kids in the United States—that's 1 in 6. In Canada it's 1 in 6 as well, which means that 1 kid on your hockey team's starting lineup doesn't have enough to eat. To put it another way, in a classroom of 24, 4 children might not have eaten breakfast on any given day. Around the world, 1 in 9 doesn't have enough food. Yet when you throw out the bruised apple in your lunch bag or don't feel like eating your dad's leftover meatloaf, it's hard to see how your food waste affects others. After all, it's not like someone else is going to eat what you don't want. But the idea that it's okay to waste food is something we need to decide is unacceptable. Right now, many of us don't think too much about this issue at all. And that has to change.

Many of us don't finish our food and are quick to toss out anything we don't want to eat.
TETRA IMAGES/GETTY IMAGES

In one month a family of four wastes...

Processed Fruit and Vegetables
10.5 lbs (4.7 kg)

Fresh Fruit and Vegetables
24 lbs (10.8 kg)

Other
12.8 lbs (5.8 kg)

Fluid Milk
22 lbs (9.9 kg)

Grains
18.5 lbs (8.3 kg)

Fats and Oils
8.60 lbs (3.9 kg)

Meat and Fish
10.4 lbs (4.7 kg)

Sweeteners
15 lbs (6.8 kg)

DATA SOURCE: NEW YORK TIMES

Too Much Food Is Tossed Away

Think of all the food the world produces as a pie—a big, delicious apple pie. Now cut it into three huge slices and throw one out. That's how much of the world's food we waste. In wealthier parts of the world, like North America and Europe, you'd have to throw away an even bigger piece of that apple pie. How is this possible? Some of the food we grow stays on farms, or on our trees because it isn't picked. Some is rejected by grocery stores because it's misshapen. Some is wasted at restaurants because portion sizes are too big and people can't finish what they order. But the largest cause of food waste might surprise you. It's us. Families waste more than grocery stores and restaurants combined.

Apple peels are delicious, but we still waste a lot in our own kitchens.
PAUL MANSFIELD PHOTOGRAPHY/ GETTY IMAGES

How Much Is Too Much?

One study looked at food-waste habits in the United States, Canada, Australia and New Zealand. Here's what people in this group of countries waste at home:

milk	20 percent
meat	22 percent
grain products	38 percent
fruits and vegetables	48 percent
seafood	50 percent

DATA SOURCE: FOOD AND AGRICULTURE ORGANIZATION 2011

Erin Silver

Too much good produce is wasted in grocery stores. But households are the biggest source of waste of all.

AANEELA/DREAMSTIME.COM

That food adds up in big ways:

- In the United States, a family of four spends $1,500 a year on food they don't eat. That's like buying five bags of groceries and throwing two in the garbage. When you add up how much most families waste, it totals more than $180 billion. You could probably buy every professional sports team in North America for that and still have money left over for a stadium hot dog!

- In the United Kingdom, people throw away up to 11 million tons (10 million metric tons) of food each year because they buy too much or don't use it all on time. A food-waste organization called Love Food Hate Waste found that every day about 20 million slices of bread are thrown away in UK homes—enough to feed 10 million people. After a year, those slices could circle the earth from pole to pole 28 times!

- Canadian households waste almost 20 million tons (18 million metric tons) of food a year, 63 percent of which could have been eaten. What does that look like? Every day Canadians waste:

470,000 heads of lettuce

1,200,000 tomatoes

2,400,000 potatoes

750,000 loaves of bread

1,225,000 apples

555,000 bananas

1,000,000 cups of milk

450,000 eggs

BITS + BITES

Finding solutions is hardly a "piece of cake." But some countries are leading the way. France is doing a *fantastique* job! The government made it illegal for grocery stores to throw away edible food. Now the country has the top spot on the Food Sustainability Index, which ranks 60 countries each year according to how much food they waste per person.

Other countries making great progress include Norway, Denmark, Japan and South Korea.

*WASTE PER PERSON PER YEAR

United States	Belgium	Canada	France
209 pounds (95.1 kg)	192 pounds (87.1 kg)	172 pounds (78.2 kg)	148 pounds (67.2 kg)

Food for Thought:
Food Waste around the World

The 2021 UN report found that the global average of food waste per person each year is about 163 pounds (73 kilograms). The exact number may vary, depending on who is measuring and how they're measuring it, but one thing is clear: we all need to cut back. Food waste is a global problem.

Experts believe that people in more developed countries are choosing to throw away food because they don't value it. Developing nations, on the other hand, don't have a way to keep food fresh for long. It goes bad before people can eat it, resulting in food waste. These countries don't have the refrigeration, transportation systems or infrastructure to avoid food waste. In other words, they don't have a choice. Imagine how the statistics would change if people in wealthier countries appreciated their food a little more.

Food for Thought:
Banker Boy Banks on Youth

José Adolfo Quisocala Condori was only 7 when he was voted mayor of his elementary school in Peru. "There were students who had trouble buying their snacks and school supplies for lack of money," said José. There were also kids who littered on the school grounds. José wanted to teach his classmates how to conserve and take care of the environment, and that's where his idea of the Bartselana Student Bank was born. Today thousands of children in his community, ages 10 to 18, participate in the program, which is now called the Cooperative Eco-bank. Whether they want to save money or need a loan, children learn how to help the planet and earn money at the same time. "Children bring in their solid waste and the value of that waste is deposited into their Visa savings account," said José. "They decide how they spend or what they do with that money." He has won many awards, including the Children's Climate Prize. He's also earned the nickname Banker Boy.

Kids all over the world are finding creative ways to help others.
COURTESY OF JOSÉ ADOLFO QUISOCALA CONDORI

Why So Much Food Gets Squandered at Home

You may be wondering why we waste so much food at home. A lot of research has been done to figure out the main causes:

- We don't feel like eating leftovers.

- We don't know how to use foods in new ways.

- The best-before, sell-by and expiry-date labels are confusing.

- We "lose" foods in the fridge and pantry and don't find them until they've gone bad.

- We aren't organized when we go to the store and end up buying too much food.

- Thanks to our busy lifestyles, we don't end up using the food we bought, even if we planned to.

- Family-sized packages of food mean that smaller families buy more than they need to save money.

Other Causes of Food Waste

Research shows that 61 percent of food that is wasted globally happens at home. Where does the rest of it happen? The UN report found that 26 percent happens in restaurants, cafeterias and food trucks. This is largely because portion sizes are too big to finish. Another 13 percent is wasted in grocery stores when food gets spoiled or becomes too old to sell according to sell-by dates. (In chapter 4 we'll talk about why these labels are confusing.)

Other organizations look at how much produce is wasted on farms. They've found that 50 percent of what's grown isn't eaten. That's because farmers grow extra in case things like the weather or bugs ruin a portion of their crops. Some isn't picked because there aren't enough people to help with the harvest—those fruits and veggies are left to rot and eventually get plowed back into the soil. Half of what isn't picked is

What a waste. Have you ever thought about what you're eating—or not eating—at home?

(LEFT) MUKHINA1/GETTY IMAGES

(TOP RIGHT) CAVAN IMAGES/GETTY IMAGES

(BOTTOM RIGHT) JOSE A. BERNAT BACETE/ GETTY IMAGES

It used to be our duty to waste as little as possible. Our attitude toward food waste has changed a lot over the years.
THE NATIONAL ARCHIVES (UNITED KINGDOM)/WIKIMEDIA COMMONS/ PUBLIC DOMAIN

still good to eat. Half of that could be sold to stores except it doesn't meet cosmetic standards. It's called **ugly food**, which means it's the "wrong" shape, size or color. Many entrepreneurs are finding new ways to use nutritious but ugly food so less goes to waste.

Too Precious to Spoil

During World Wars I and II, food shortages meant families had to **ration**, or conserve, their food. Food was expensive, and some ingredients were hard to find. While soldiers were fighting overseas, people at home made food stretch as far as it could go. Nothing went to waste. They used stale bread or potato peels to thicken soup. Chicken fat was used as cooking oil—some people even ate fat sandwiches. Chicken bones and vegetable scraps made soup stock. People in the United States, Canada, the United Kingdom and elsewhere grew victory gardens—vegetables in their yards, empty lots and public parks—to add to their food supply. But in the years after the war, there was plenty of food. People became more wasteful. Now Americans toss 70 percent more food than they did even a few decades ago.

FOOD-WASTE HERO
Everything Has a Purpose

Dr. Enrique Salmón is an author, Indigenous leader from the Rarámuri tribe in Mexico and professor of ethnic studies at California State University, East Bay. He spends a lot of time thinking about the connections between the climate crisis and the way Indigenous people eat.

"Traditional Native peoples hold the natural world in high regard. To us, everything is alive," says Enrique. "We feel we are directly related to and share energy and breath with everything around us. It would be deeply disrespectful to gather plants, to fish or to hunt the life around us only to use a small fraction of what we have hunted or gathered."

In his home, Enrique keeps the carrot greens to flavor soups and stews. He does the same with garlic and onions. Every part of an animal is useful too—and not just for food. The bones of large animals can be used to make tools or parts of musical instruments and can even be dried and ground into a meal to be added to garden soils. Fur and hides are used for clothing and shelter. "Even the skins and innards of fish are returned to the earth and the rivers to provide food for aquatic life and to the creatures that occupy the soil below our feet," says Enrique.

He wants people to think about food differently and show respect for all living things. He believes we should all act responsibly and consider how our actions and choices are going to affect everything around us.

Dr. Enrique Salmón thinks about the planet when he eats. He doesn't let anything go to waste.
FLAVIA MORLACHETTI/GETTY IMAGES
(INSET) COURTESY OF DR. SALMÓN

Some people search through dumpsters behind grocery stores and find a lot of perfectly good food that's been thrown away.

GROGL/SHUTTERSTOCK.COM

Tristram Stuart has traveled the world and discovered just how big a global problem food waste has become.

COURTESY OF TRISTRAM STUART

Dumpsters Filled with Food

Tristram Stuart is a food-waste activist. He's famous for showing us that food waste is a gigantic problem around the world. His life as a food-waste hero began with his pigs. Wanting to fatten them up, he spoke to local farmers, butchers, bakers and grocers in his hometown of Sussex, England, to see if they had any food scraps. It turned out they had lots of food for Tristram's pigs...perfectly good food fit for humans. Just 15 years old at the time, he began looking in supermarket dumpsters headed for the landfill. He was shocked to find the dumpsters full of delicious, healthy food. He thought there must be better things to do with food than waste it. Tristram did some homework. He helped others see that good, fresh food was being wasted on a colossal scale. Now in his 40s, Tristram teaches people how to reduce food waste—and what will happen if we don't. Many others have joined the cause. It turns out the planet needs our help.

Gigi Martínez Gracida is a young activist in Mexico. She loves helping children and the planet.

COURTESY OF GIGI MARTÍNEZ GRACIDA

Food for Thought:
Cleaning Up the Planet and Filling Up Tummies

Many families don't worry about whether the food in their fridge will spoil—they worry about whether they will have anything to eat at all. A teen activist in Oaxaca, Mexico, named Gigi Martínez Gracida helps hungry rural schoolchildren. She collects plastic bottles and sells the recyclables to buy them food. Her program supports about 140 children. "I'm helping to reduce environmental pollution, and with the money obtained, food is bought so that the rural schoolchildren always have their breakfast," says Gigi. "This helps them achieve a better performance in their education." Gigi sits on many international youth committees, speaks at conferences around the world and has received lots of awards for her outstanding service, including a Global Peace and Humanitarian Award in 2021. With so many children in need, this teen is just getting started.

You'd think it would be impossible to eat entirely from food left in dumpsters, but one couple did it—and made a movie about it!

JUST EAT IT: A FOOD WASTE STORY/
FOODWASTEMOVIE.COM

Food for Thought:
Watch This!

Grant Baldwin and Jen Rustemeyer were shocked by the amount of perfectly good food that gets thrown away every day—food that is edible but not used, is ugly or is approaching its expiry date. The Canadian couple decided to do an experiment. For six months could they live off perfectly edible food that was being discarded? They began sorting through garbage bins. Their effort was featured in a documentary they directed and produced called *Just Eat It: A Food Waste Story*. The film gave audiences an eye-opening look at a massive problem—a problem that is especially shocking considering how many families are food insecure. "Making this film we thought we were going to be exposing industry food waste, but it really turned into…how much the individual plays a part and how much the average household is wasting," said Grant in an interview. He and Jen started cooking more, using their senses rather than the expiry label, and added an "eat me first" bin so they could see the food that needed to be eaten before it expired.

Two
Food Waste Feeds Global Warming

Cutting food waste is one of the most important things we can do to curb global warming. And that helps everyone on the planet in a big way.
WESTEND61/GETTY IMAGES

Imagine you've spent hours cooking a big meal for your family. Let's say you've made cheddar-broccoli soup to start, then roast beef for dinner and chocolate cake for dessert. People sit down to eat, take a few bites and say, "I don't like this" or "I'm full." The rest of the meal gets thrown away. *Harrumph!* What a waste! It took ages to plan, shop for and cook the meal, not to mention how expensive the ingredients were to buy.

This might not sound familiar to you—that was a pretty lavish meal!—but the truth is, many people waste food without realizing the real cost. That's because the biggest expense isn't felt in our bank accounts. When we throw out food, the planet suffers the consequences.

Food for Thought:
You Can Make a Big Difference by Cutting Food Waste

A book called *Drawdown* lists 100 things people can do to tackle global warming. Reducing food waste is third. In other words, eating the food we buy and wasting as little as we can is one of the top three things we can do to slow the climate crisis. If we cut global food waste in half, carbon emissions could decrease by 70.53 gigatons by 2050. How big is a **gigaton**? One gigaton equals more than the weight of six million blue whales or more than a hundred million African elephants. Translation? Cutting food waste can really help the planet!

Jaime Vladimir Espinosa Herrera is a young man with a big idea—planting trees in exchange for food. It's a win-win.
COURTESY OF JAIME VLADIMIR ESPINOSA HERRERA

Food for Thought:

Trees for Food

The COVID-19 pandemic caused thousands of people to lose their jobs, making it hard for many families to afford food. Jaime Vladimir Espinosa Herrera couldn't let that happen in his community. He established a project called Árboles por Alimento, or Trees for Food. The 23-year-old student from Zacatecas, Mexico, began trading trees, such as pines and mesquite, in exchange for food and supplies, which he then gave to vulnerable families. Tree owners then plant the trees to reforest the land. So far the project has delivered more than 1,000 trees and helped over 500 families. After a forest fire charred the land in an area called Cerro de la Bufa, Jaime used the same idea to reforest that area. The trees-for-food idea has been copied in other communities and even the Mexican government has gotten involved. It's a great way to help the hungry and the environment.

The Real Cost of Growing Food

Land ·

A lot of land is used to grow food that's wasted. And that's not good. Here's how the trouble happens. Forests are cut down to clear land for crops and animals. Now those trees can't absorb *carbon dioxide* to clean the air. Many species of animals lose their homes. Deforestation causes 150 to 200 animal, plant and insect species to become extinct every day—all to grow food we don't think twice about wasting.

A lot of land is cleared to raise cattle. We lose trees and animal habitats and produce more emissions. We're creating a big environmental footprint, and we add to it when we throw away food.
(TOP) HELDER FARIA/GETTY IMAGES
(BOTTOM) LUCAS NINNO/GETTY IMAGES

Water

Growing produce and raising animals uses a lot of water. This chart shows how much water is needed to raise the roast beef you didn't feel like eating and grow the broccoli for the soup you poured down the drain. The water needed to produce the amount of food North Americans waste in a year could fill seven million Olympic-sized swimming pools.

To put it another way, the amount of water needed to make one hamburger is what you'd use if you took a 90-minute shower. Almost 220 gallons (1,000 liters) of water is wasted when you pour one glass of milk down the drain.

BITS + BITES

Every year American shoppers, businesses and farmers spend $218 billion growing, processing, transporting and disposing of food that's never even eaten.

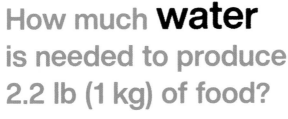

How much **water** is needed to produce 2.2 lb (1 kg) of food?

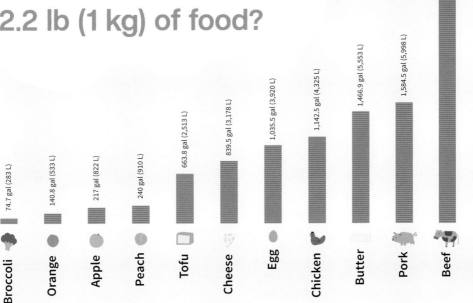

Food	Water
Tomato	56.5 gal (214 L)
Broccoli	74.7 gal (283 L)
Orange	140.8 gal (533 L)
Apple	217 gal (822 L)
Peach	240 gal (910 L)
Tofu	663.8 gal (2,513 L)
Cheese	839.5 gal (3,178 L)
Egg	1,035.5 gal (3,920 L)
Chicken	1,142.5 gal (4,325 L)
Butter	1,466.9 gal (5,553 L)
Pork	1,584.5 gal (5,998 L)
Beef	4,072 gal (15,415 L)

DATA SOURCE: WATER FOOTPRINT NETWORK

A lot of our food travels long distances to end up on our plates. Sometimes the sticker on a food item tells you where it's from.

TADA IMAGES/SHUTTERSTOCK.COM

Energy

Getting food from farms to our fridges takes a lot of energy. Think about all the gas and electricity needed to run farm machines and then truck food from farms to processing plants and from there to distribution centers and supermarkets. At every stage, food needs to be refrigerated. Then we use our cars to drive to stores and restaurants and home again. A University of Oxford study found that food production causes 25 percent of all greenhouse gas emissions. When we waste food, it adds so much greenhouse gas to the atmosphere it's like driving 41 million cars for a year without stopping.

Trash

Americans throw out enough food each year to fill 13 football stadiums. In fact, food waste is the number one item in US landfills. These big, stinky heaps of trash cost the planet too. When food rots in a landfill, it releases **methane,** which is even more powerful as a heat-trapping gas than carbon dioxide. Even if we put our food scraps in the green bin for **composting**, they create methane when they decompose. And don't forget the garbage trucks that collect our food waste—they cause emissions too. All of our garbage has a big impact on the climate crisis.

Putting Food Waste on the Map

If food waste was a country, it would be the third-largest emitter of greenhouse gases after China and the United States. Some scientists say that if we stopped wasting food, we could reduce our greenhouse gas emissions by 6 to 8 percent, if not more. That's actually a large percentage.

The Link between the Planet and Your Plate

All foods have a *carbon footprint,* or a cost to the environment. Certain foods, like fruits and vegetables, take less water and resources to grow than animal-based products do. Meat and dairy products, like steak, cheese and ice cream, have a bigger environmental cost. They make up more than half of greenhouse gas emissions caused by food production but are only part of our daily diet. Cutting back on animal-based foods could reduce your carbon footprint from food by 66 percent a year. But you don't have to be a *vegan* to make a difference.

Cutting back on meat even once a week can help the planet.
NICK DAVID/GETTY IMAGES

BITS + BITES

Curious about your diet's carbon footprint? You can calculate the carbon footprint of your favorite foods by searching for "carbon footprint calculator" online.

Going to local farmers' markets is fun and a great way to eat local, healthy foods from nearby farms.

MARTINEDOUCET/GETTY IMAGES

A few small changes in how you shop and what you buy can make a difference. Here's what you can do to effect change.

Eat local

About 15 percent of food in the United States comes from somewhere else. In North America, your groceries may travel 1,500 to 2,500 miles (2,400 to 4,000 kilometers) before you buy them. Transporting food this far creates a lot of emissions. That's why some people choose to eat local. They call themselves *locavores*. This means they buy food from nearby producers rather than from faraway farms. Lots of restaurants offer an "eat local" menu, featuring food grown or made closer to home. If you're dining out or ordering takeout, ask your parents or guardians to order from restaurants close to home to reduce your carbon footprint. Maybe you can even walk there together!

Shop at farmers' markets ·····················

Ever notice how much plastic packaging is involved when you buy fresh foods from the supermarket? Lots! Plastic keeps food fresh and in good condition, but it's a big problem for the planet. About a third of the plastic the world uses each year ends up polluting our land and oceans. It releases toxins or entangles marine life. You can shop for farm-fresh fruits and veggies at local farmers' markets instead, where there's less packaging. You'll also be supporting small family-run farms and eating *seasonal foods*. That's because farmers' markets sell only fruits and veggies that are in season, which means you can enjoy the freshest, tastiest strawberries in June and the sweetest, juiciest grapes in September, when they are ripe.

Look for what's in season when you're shopping. You'll get fresh fruits and veggies when they're the tastiest.
ARTMARIE/GETTY IMAGES

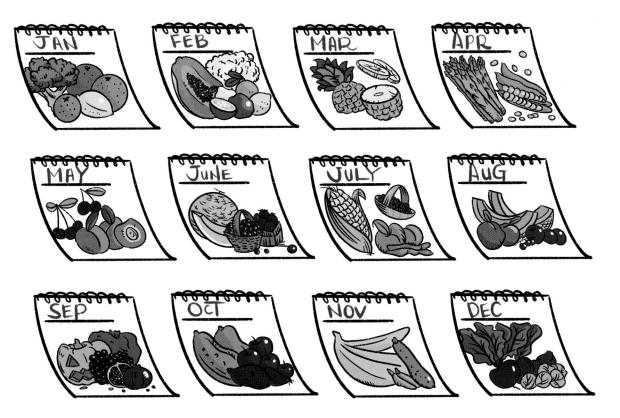

Sometimes you might buy these foods "out of season" at a grocery store. This means you can eat strawberries in January, but they practically need a passport to make it across the world and onto your plate. Just how far do your fruits travel? You might not realize it but, depending on where you live, your apples can travel as far as 1,555 miles (2,502 kilometers) to a depot where they can be purchased by a grocery store, compared to 77 miles (124 kilometers) to a farmers' market. And your tomatoes might be shipped 1,369 miles (2,203 kilometers) versus 117 miles (188 kilometers) to the nearest farmers' market. Buying food that has traveled less distance is one of the reasons why farmers' markets are popular.

Try a meatless meal

Raising animals contributes more greenhouse gas emissions than all the transportation in the world combined. That's because animal farming creates a lot of emissions. Some cows can release 132 to 264 gallons (500 to 999 liters) of gas a day. All these gases trap heat in the atmosphere and contribute to global warming. Raising animals requires a lot of water too. It takes about 1,850 gallons (7,003 liters) of water to produce a pound (about half a kilogram) of beef. For these reasons, some people choose to become **vegetarians**, with a diet that doesn't contain meat. A lot of people are trying **plant-based foods**. These foods aren't made with animal products. Instead they're made with fruits, vegetables, some nuts and beans, which are more environmentally friendly. Even reducing how much meat you eat can help. Some families like the idea of meatless Mondays. It's a great way to get more veggies into your growing body. Others eat less red meat and more pork or chicken. If everyone in the United States gave up red meat one day a week, greenhouse gas emissions would decrease by 0.3 percent each year. It might not sound like a lot, but every bite helps.

There are lots of great plant-based foods to enjoy.
WESTEND61/GETTY IMAGES

Look for recipes you can make at home. It's a great way to try new, healthy foods.

Even milk has a carbon footprint, but dairy farmers are finding ways to reduce its impact.

BITS + BITES

Raising cattle uses 28 times more land and 11 times more water, and produces 5 times more greenhouse gas emissions, than raising pigs or chickens does.

Mooo-ving toward Change

Ranchers and dairy farmers know that their jobs are affecting the planet. The Dairy Farmers of Canada was one of the first organizations to change its practices to help the planet. Now Canadian milk is made with one of the lowest carbon footprints in the world. That's because new research taught farmers how to better care for their cows. These cows are living longer and making more milk. The fewer the cows, the less the effect on the planet. While new research and methods will continue to improve how farmers operate, look at how things have changed in your lifetime:

- In 2011 producing a jug of milk created more carbon dioxide than it does today.

- Farmers use 6 percent less water and 11 percent less land to make a carton of milk than they used to.

- Better *supply-chain management* means that farmers make the amount of milk that's needed rather than too much. Now there's no crying over spoiled milk.

- Many farmers use a *biodigester* to turn the methane from cow manure into electricity.

- Better fertilizers without harmful chemicals help reduce *groundwater contamination*.

FOOD-WASTE HERO:

"Meat" Kay Cornelius

Kay Cornelius is an organic rancher and president of Panorama Meats in Denver, a collective of some 50 ranchers in the US grasslands from California to Wisconsin. Kay thinks about how cows affect the planet every step of the way. Instead of using other land to grow food for her cattle, Panorama cattle eat the grass in their pastures. The grass is healthy for cows to eat and can't be used for anything else. As the cows move from pasture to pasture, the grass has time to regrow naturally. Panorama cows drink from ponds, streams or wells—ranchers don't need to use extra water. The animals aren't given any hormones, and the grass isn't treated with pesticides, which is good for wildlife and the soil.

Panorama Meats works with the Audubon Society, a nonprofit organization in the United States that helps protect birds and their habitat. Kay herself eats a lot of vegetables and a little bit of organic beef. "Our meat is very nutritious and highly dense," she says. "You can get a ton of protein, vitamins and omega 3s, and you don't have to eat a lot of it—you just have to eat the right amount."

Sustainable ranchers like Kay Cornelius think about how they can help the planet when they're raising their cows.
CANDICE VIVIEN FOR PANORAMA ORGANIC GRASS-FED MEATS

Food for Thought:
Sustainable Cattle Ranching around the World

Too much forest land has been destroyed to make space for cattle ranching, and it's led to an increase in greenhouse gas emissions. These changes have affected rainfall patterns and made extreme weather, like storms, more common. Major organizations are stepping in to help farmers affected by the climate crisis. For example, the Colombian government is working with the World Bank and others on the Sustainable Cattle Ranching project.

It's been a success for Colombian farmer Maria Gladys Apolinar. She's been practicing ***silvopastoral farming***, which uses nature to create healthier livestock, better soil and fewer greenhouse gas emissions. Maria added a cocoa crop around her land so her cows, chickens and rabbits could have shade. New hedges are a "living fence" and newly planted meadow buttercups are high-protein snacks for her cows—sort of like a vending machine. She moves her livestock around her land so her plants can regrow. And she learned to use manure to create organic fertilizer. "Nothing goes to waste here," she says. These changes are paying off. Milk production has increased seven times in just a few years. Now others in Latin America and beyond are thirsty to try sustainable farming too.

Beyond Beef

While some ranchers are thinking about how to be more sustainable, other companies are looking at different solutions. Beyond Meat uses plant-based ingredients to make products that taste like meat but use less of Earth's resources. It's just one of many companies working on ways to help people find more environmentally friendly diets. The Plant Based Foods Association represents hundreds of plant-based food companies. They say eating more plants is also better for our bodies. Their research has found that by using land to grow plants rather than to raise animals, we could feed more people with the same amount of land.

People around the world are realizing that what goes on our plates affects the planet. Many are even starting to make changes. But it's not nearly enough to solve the food-waste crisis. We know that millions of people don't have enough to eat. We also know that producing more food isn't the answer. We need to prevent food waste in the first place. And we need to make sure that the food we have is being eaten by people. Nobody should go hungry when there's plenty of food for everyone. It's a matter of justice—***food justice***. The next chapter looks at new ideas and innovations that are getting food to the hungry.

The Landworkers Alliance and others in the UK demonstrate at the Good Food March. It's not fair that some people have too much to eat and others don't have enough, especially when there's plenty to go around.
GOOD FOOD GOOD FARMING/
GOODFOODGOODFARMING.EU

Three
Food for All

SOURCE: EPA

Food Recovery Hierarchy

Source Reduction
Reduce surplus food generated

Feed Hungry People
Donate extra food to food banks, soup kitchens and shelters

Feed Animals
Divert food scraps to animal food

Industrial Uses
Provide waste oils for rendering and fuel conversion and food scraps for digestion to recover energy

Composting
Create nutrient-rich soil amendment

Landfill/Incineration
Last resort to disposal

Most Preferred

Least Preferred

When experts talk about *food recovery* or *food rescue,* they're talking about how we get edible food to people who need it instead of letting it go to waste. After all, everyone should be able to have fresh, healthy, culturally appropriate foods (foods typically eaten in different cultures), especially when there's enough for everyone. This is called *food justice.*

Governments, start-ups, nonprofits, restaurants and grocery stores are trying to help. They're finding ways to get good food to people who need it. And they're reducing food waste in the process.

Governments Can Help

France wastes the least amount of food in the world. Part of the reason for that is a law passed by the government in 2016 to help reduce food waste. The law requires grocery stores to donate edible food. Grocery-store managers caught tossing out food could be fined or go to jail. The government's Inglorious Fruits and Vegetables campaign also brings attention to food waste.

In Norway the government is helping people understand use-by and best-before dates, and grocery stores are donating and discounting foods before they go bad. Denmark is also a leader in Europe. The country has more programs to reduce food waste than any other country in Europe. The Danes have been able to reduce food waste by 25 percent. A campaign called Stop Spild Af Mad, or Stop Wasting Food, has received a lot of media attention. The campaign aims to make people feel good about reducing food waste. For example, doggie bags are now called goodie bags, which means Danes are no longer embarrassed to have restaurants pack up their leftovers. A supermarket called WeFood is Denmark's first grocery store to sell food that otherwise would have been wasted. People from all walks of life can buy surplus food at prices 30 to 50 percent lower than at regular supermarkets.

Since 2016 Seoul, South Korea, has reduced its food waste by 300 tons (272 metric tons) per day. Citizens there have to pay a fee based on how much food they waste. Special bins equipped with scales calculate the volume of waste, and residents are billed accordingly. Waste can be composted (for a smaller fee) or it can be used as animal feed or turned into energy (more on this in chapter 4). South Koreans have been able to reduce their daily food waste to the weight of a couple of grapefruits per family.

China has taken another approach. Restaurants can be fined up to 10,000 yuan (about US $1,500) for encouraging customers to order too much food. There's also a ban on TV shows or videos that show people stuffing their faces. The fine for that is a maximum of 100,000 yuan (more than US $15,000). It's China's way of ensuring there's enough food to feed its population of 1.4 billion people. It also promotes a healthy, frugal lifestyle.

Food for Thought:
An Open Challenge

In 2010 the United States Environmental Protection Agency (EPA) launched a Food Recovery Challenge. The challenge raises awareness about the impact of food waste. It also recognizes food-waste heroes for reducing food waste, helping communities and protecting the planet. Many amazing ideas and initiatives have received funding. Most important, they've helped people and the planet by

- preventing over 18,000 tons (16,329 metric tons) of wasted food from being created;
- donating approximately 317,000 tons (287, 578 metric tons) of food;
- anaerobically digesting nearly 47,000 tons (42,638 metric tons) of food; and
- composting more than 269,000 tons (244,033 metric tons) of food.

Recently Canada launched a similar program. Called the Food Waste Reduction Challenge, it comes with $20 million in funding for the best ideas. One company was recognized for finding a way to turn okara, the pulp left over from producing tofu or soy milk, into healthy flour, noodles and baked goods. Another company found a way to transform upcycled fruits and vegetables into dehydrated powder, frozen cubes and purees. This makes them last longer so they don't go to waste right away. Keep up the good work, warriors!

NO WASTE.

second harvest

NO HUNGER.

DELIVERING GOOD, SURPLUS FOOD
TO PEOPLE IN NEED

Lori Nikkel's goals at Second Harvest are to get food to people who need it and ensure that people are wasting as little as possible.

BITS + BITES

Since 1985 Second Harvest has rescued and delivered more than 177 million pounds (80 million kilograms) of food and stopped over 75 million pounds (34 million kilograms) of greenhouse gas equivalents from heating the planet.

Smart Thinking

Second Harvest is the largest food-rescue, or food-recovery, organization in Canada. Staff also do a lot of research on food waste. "When you look at the amount of food that's wasted, it's shameful," says Second Harvest CEO Lori Nikkel.

The organization's research shows that 58 percent of all food produced for Canadians is wasted as it moves from farm to table. Thirty-two percent of that is completely avoidable and is enough to fill a freight train stretching from Ottawa to Winnipeg. "We should be eating it," says Lori. At her house, she stocks only the food she needs and uses common sense to decide if food is bad. And she reuses as much as she can.

At work she's busy helping others. Second Harvest has an app that connects farmers, grocery stores and restaurants with charities. The nonprofit then puts food on trucks, planes and trains and sends it from coast to coast to coast. Second Harvest teaches Canadians how to measure food waste and manage it. It offers online classes on how to decode expiry dates, store food in a way that makes it last longer and cook to reduce waste.

"We have a culture that thinks it's okay to create waste," says Lori. "Best-before dates are a huge contributor to food waste. We need to avoid waste in the first place."

Best-before labels are confusing. The best way to tell if food is good to eat is by using your senses. And your common sense.
PETER DAZELEY/GETTY IMAGES

Food for Thought:
What's the Problem with Best-before Dates?

Many of us think best-before dates indicate when food expires. But only five foods (think baby formula and nutritional supplements) have actual expiry dates. A best-before date is when foods are at their highest freshness or quality—when a pie crust is flakiest or a cake is most moist, for example. It doesn't mean the food is bad to eat after that date. Without laws to make it easy for us to understand labels, food manufacturers can put dates on food packages that don't tell you when food is spoiled. This means we throw out food without smelling it, tasting it or seeing that it's actually curdled, moldy or rotten.

Gleaning from Farms

Lots of volunteers are *gleaning*. This means they are picking unharvested fruits or vegetables from farms or even people's backyard trees to help get good, fresh food to people who need it. Jonathan Bloom is an environmental journalist and expert on food waste. He also loves to glean in North Carolina, where he lives with his family. "Gleaning is one of the best ways to spend a few hours or an entire day," says Jonathan, author of *American Wasteland: How America Throws Away Nearly Half of Its Food (and What We Can Do About It)*.

Gleaning opened his eyes to the amount of food that goes to waste on farms. "Farmers plant more than they need in case something goes wrong with the field or crop," he explains. "This way they have enough to sell to grocery stores."

Farmers also know that grocery stores won't want to buy produce that looks less than perfect. "They need extra because some produce will be the 'wrong' shape, size or color," says Jonathan.

Sometimes food gets left on farms because there aren't enough people to pick it. All of this leads to extra produce that can be gleaned and given to those in need. On a recent harvest Jonathan and his fellow volunteers were able to donate thousands of pounds of sweet potatoes to food banks. They stopped them from rotting and going to waste. You can glean too. Ask your parents to help you find a nearby farm that needs volunteers.

BITS + BITES

A popular gelato shop in California called Ecco Un Poco unintentionally helped rescue fruit when customers stopped by with some peaches and figs from their trees. The shop turned the fruit into a seasonal gelato flavor for everyone to enjoy. After all, fruit doesn't have to look perfect to taste delicious!

Food for Thought:
The Invention of Baby Carrots

Grocery stores won't buy "ugly" carrots. But this is actually how baby carrots got their start. Rather than throw out ugly carrots, California farmer Mike Yurosek realized he could peel and cut them into cute little carrots to reduce waste. Today more than half of all carrots sold are baby carrots. Now other companies are using imperfect produce in new ways. Maybe you've had it in freshly pressed juice, smoothies or whole as part of an "ugly fruit box" delivered to your home.

This carrot might be ugly, but it's still delicious and nutritious.
UGLY CARROT: KSENIYA OVCHINNIKOVA/GETTY IMAGES
BABY CARROTS: BWFOLSOM/GETTY IMAGES

FOOD-WASTE HERO:

Introducing Rick Nahmias, Founder and CEO of Food Forward

Rick Nahmias was walking around his neighborhood in Los Angeles in 2009 and couldn't believe his eyes. "There was a huge amount of produce on trees in people's front and backyards that was never used—grapefruits, pomegranates, avocados and more," says Rick. "All of these mature trees were being ignored and yet there was a need at food pantries. They had **shelf-stable foods** like pasta and canned goods, but they weren't getting the fresh supplies they needed."

Rick gathered his friends and picked fruit from neighborhood trees (Los Angeles County actually has over one million residential fruit trees!). That first time, they donated 800 pounds (363 kilograms) of citrus fruit that otherwise would have rotted. While picking, Rick climbed up a fruit tree. "In that moment I got 15 feet (4.5 meters) high and I saw how much fruit is on trees. I suddenly got a vision of how big this could be."

Since he founded Food Forward, his organization has grown. It has donated 185 million pounds (almost 84 million kilograms) of fruit and vegetables to people who need it. By doing this, Food Forward prevented 56,000 tons (51,000 metric tons) of carbon dioxide from entering the air, fed millions of people and engaged thousands of volunteers. Recently Rick invested in a gigantic refrigerated warehouse and named it Produce Pit Stop. Food is stored there and given to food agencies across southern California and tribal lands in Arizona and New Mexico. Thanks to organizations like Food Forward—nonprofits that operate across North America—people get to eat fresh foods they normally don't find at food banks.

Rick Nahmias (opposite) began Food Forward to rescue fresh fruits from local trees. Now his organization redistributes healthy foods to people who wouldn't normally get to eat it.

(OPPOSITE) COURTESY OF FOOD FORWARD

(BELOW) ANNA EVTUKHOVA/DREAMSTIME.COM

Caue Suplicy makes healthy snacks from bananas that would otherwise go to waste.

Upcycling and Peeling Good

BITS + BITES

Recycling turns broken-down waste into another product or material. Often the quality of that product or material isn't as good as the original. Upcycling takes waste and repurposes it into something better.

Many entrepreneurs are turning a problem into a product. They are using leftover ingredients and imperfect produce to create other things people can eat—things like crackers, bread, protein powder, banana snacks and even beer. (Remember Tristram from chapter 1? His company, Toast Ale, turns leftover bread into beer!) The idea is so popular that the Upcycled Food Association says there are now more than 400 upcycled products on US store shelves.

Caue Suplicy helped get the upcycling movement started in the United States more than a decade ago. A triathlete from Brazil, he wanted to bring a popular childhood banana treat to a new audience. When he came across a huge supply of imperfect bananas in Latin America, he got an "appealing" idea. He began upcycling the fruit into delicious sweet and salty snacks. All those bananas would have been wasted, all because they were a little too long, too short or a bit too ripe. Today his company, Barnana, helps rescue food and ensures that Indigenous banana farmers in the Amazon have extra income from selling imperfect bananas. He's also creating delicious snacks everyone can enjoy, whether they are triathletes or tricycle riders.

There are so many great ways to use bananas—call it upcycling!
(BANANA CHIPS) BERGAMONT/GETTY IMAGES
(SMOOTHIE) ANGELA KOTSELL/
GETTY IMAGES

BITS + BITES

You might already be upcycling! Do you freeze ripened fruit and use it in smoothies? That's great! There's even more you can do. Look online for recipe ideas or buy products with the Upcycled Food Association seal.

There's an App for That

Josh Domingues was living above a grocery store in Ontario when the idea for a new app came to him. Upset when his sister, a chef, had to throw out $4,000 worth of food, he decided to tackle a huge problem within the industry. Grocery stores are left with tons of food that's getting close to its best-before date. It's all thrown in the garbage. Grocers have been trying to find ways to reduce waste by keeping food fresher for longer or donating it, but a lot is still sent to the landfill. Josh wondered if he could create a phone app that would enable people to buy food nearing its best-before date at a discount and then pick it up in-store. That way he could help get food to people who needed it while also helping the planet. His app Flashfood was born. It's a win-win for people and the planet.

Food on the Move

Jasmine Crowe is not about to let kids go hungry, especially when she can do something about it. "Hunger is not an issue of scarcity; it's a matter of logistics," says the founder and CEO of Goodr Inc. She created a real-time food-rescue app that works a lot like Uber or Lyft. Restaurants, hospitals, schools or individual chefs can use the Goodr app to call a driver. The driver will pick up extra food and deliver it to shelters, seniors' centers, food pantries and soup kitchens—places where people need food. Every year 33 million tons (30 million metric tons) of good food are wasted in the United States—and it costs the country about $1.3 billion to dispose of the waste. Meanwhile, one in seven people are hungry. That number is one in three for Black and Hispanic kids. Thanks to Goodr, lots of people are getting good food right away—food that would have ended up in the trash.

Since the start of the COVID-19 pandemic in 2020, Goodr has helped feed families in several cities, including Atlanta, Los Angeles, Seattle and Washington, DC, by holding pop-up food markets. The markets provided healthy food options to hundreds of families, helping Goodr fill stomachs and meet its mission—feed more, waste less.

Kids suffering from food insececurity can get healthy food fast thanks to ideas like Goodr.

GOODLIFESTUDIO/GETTY IMAGES

Growing your own food makes you appreciate it more.

(LEFT) SONYA FARRELL/GETTY IMAGES
(RIGHT) COURTESY OF BOWERY PROJECT

Planting a Community Garden

Another great way to teach people to waste less while getting wholesome foods into hungry tummies is to grow a garden. While it's not a new idea (remember those victory gardens?), it's something many kids today might not think about trying—especially as a way to help solve the food-waste problem. Many organizations have sprouted up to do just this. Bowery Project is a not-for-profit organization that has been teaching people in urban neighborhoods around Toronto how to grow vegetables and herbs. Gardens are mobile—planted in movable containers that can be carried from one vacant lot to another.

Rachel Kimel is passionate about Bowery Project. She helped cofound it in 2013. "When you're involved in the effort of growing food, you appreciate its value and you're less likely to waste it," she says.

If you see potatoes only in a plastic bag, you have no idea how they were grown or how they got there. But when you get your hands in the dirt, "you see how long it takes to grow a carrot, how much care and effort is involved, and you can taste, touch and smell food as it grows," she says. "It makes people more willing to try a pea on the vine, bite into a tomato or use herbs in cooking."

There are other benefits too. Gardening is a great way to get outside, save money and be more connected to your food. "Being productive and doing something that has purpose and value is also great for our mental health," says Rachel.

Now those are words to savor, especially since growing food and appreciating its worth help people and the planet. But when some food still goes uneaten, other kinds of experts, such as scientists, businesspeople and school officials, are finding ways to help too.

Do you have a garden at home, at school or in the community? Maybe you can start one with your family, friends or classmates.

ANDRES BARRIONUEVO LOPEZ/GETTY IMAGES

Four
Hungry for Change

Sometimes my kids come home from school with food they didn't get to or simply couldn't eat. There were some raisins, a half-eaten apple and a banana peel in their lunch bags just the other day. But it turns out there's a lot we can do with leftovers that we humans can't eat. In fact, these bits can still be used. This is called **sustainable food management**. Big cities and grocery-store chains, baseball stadiums, universities, middle schools and even small pig sanctuaries are participating, and you can get involved too.

Feeding Animals

Some animals can eat our food scraps. Pigs have stomachs that can digest these foods better than other animals can. That's why places with tons of food waste are sending their edible leftovers to pig farmers. Rutgers University in New Jersey sends about 1.125 tons (1 metric ton) per day of food

Giving our leftover foods to animals is a great way to make sure healthy fruits and veggies don't go to waste.
WIHARJA/SHUTTERSTOCK.COM

scraps from its dining halls to nearby Pinter Farms, where hogs and cattle have been enjoying students' leftovers for nearly five decades.

On the other side of the United States there's another long-time food-recovery partnership. For about 50 years, MGM Resorts International in Las Vegas sent its food waste to RC Farms. All that leftover shrimp cocktail, prime rib and sushi from the buffets fed about 2,500 pigs a year before the farm owner retired. Once the pigs even ate two-thirds of a 131,000-pound (59,420-kilogram) birthday cake!

More Than Slop

The World Wildlife Fund says that 30 percent of what's fed to livestock around the world today is food scraps. In the United States, about 10 percent of extra food from grocery stores or manufacturing plants is fed to animals. But another 14.7 million tons (13.3 million metric tons) of food waste could also be sent to farms. Yet because of outbreaks of diseases like mad cow and foot-and-mouth, laws limit whether food scraps in the form of "slop" can be fed to animals. It all depends on where you live.

Of course, to make sure food is safe for animals to eat, it needs to be properly treated. That's why food scraps are ground down and cooked at high temperatures at large processing facilities before being fed to animals. Feeding scraps to livestock prevents food waste from ending up in the landfill. It also means that instead of using more land, water and energy to grow food to feed animals, they can eat food that's already made and would otherwise end up in the garbage. Feeding animals makes good business sense too. The cost of donating food to local farms can be cheaper than paying to have it hauled to a landfill. Companies are saving money, helping animals and slowing global warming, all at the same time.

BITS + BITES

One study showed that about 4.4 million acres (1.78 million hectares) of land in Europe could be saved by feeding pigs treated, recycled food scraps instead of clearing land to grow food just for them.

Food for Thought:
Oink You for the Food!

Kirsten Duggan is the owner of Sweet Acres Pig Sanctuary in Stouffville, ON. Kirsten has almost a dozen potbellied pigs. Little goes to waste at Sweet Acres—or at nearby grocery stores! She's grateful for all the local shops that give her leftover salads, broccoli, spinach, kale and all sorts of greens so she can feed her pigs. "Our pigs get all the vitamins and minerals they need through these foods, as well as apples and carrots," says Kirsten. "When visitors come, they also bring their extra celery. It's a great way to make use of healthy foods that aren't going to be eaten by people."

Kirsten Duggan's pigs get lots of fresh foods, like celery and apples, from visitors and the community.
COURTESY OF KIRSTEN DUGGAN

Anaerobic Digestion in Action

Whole Foods uses the Grind2Energy system in their stores. It grinds food waste that can't be donated or repurposed.

The waste that is produced is then sent to an anaerobic digester and processed.

That process generates renewable energy for electricity and heat.

Food for Thought:
She Sells Seashells

The Bellagio Hotel and Casino in Las Vegas made waves recently with its oyster-shell recycling program. Instead of sending their shells to the landfill, the hotel's restaurants donated them to help replenish oyster habitats and improve water quality in Chesapeake Bay. That's because oysters are natural water purifiers that remove pollutants in water, improving its quality. Now that's a "shell" of an idea!

The Power of Food Waste

Did you know that food waste can be turned into power and electricity? Big grocers, hotels, universities and stadiums are sending food that can't be donated or repurposed to **anaerobic digestion** facilities. There, special machines heat and break down organic matter like food and turn it into **renewable energy** or **biogas**. This liquid can heat homes and provide electricity. It can even be used to power certain cars.

With a goal to chop food waste in half by 2030, Whole Foods is off to a good start. As of 2021, the grocery chain had diverted more than 25 million pounds (11.3 million kilograms) of food waste from landfills, prevented nearly 9,900 tons (9,000 metric tons) of carbon dioxide from entering the atmosphere and made enough energy to power over 2,500 homes for a month, thanks to its anaerobic-digestion efforts.

High-Tech Power Plants

Metro Vancouver was one of the first cities in Canada to encourage food retailers to reduce food waste. Whatever isn't eaten can be sent to its high-tech waste-treatment plant that converts food waste into biofuel and fertilizer. One of the biggest operations in the United States is the Wastewater Reclamation facility in Des Moines, Iowa. At last count, it had six 2.7-million-gallon (10,220-cubic-meter) anaerobic digesters. The facility processes over 60 truckloads a day of fats, grease and food waste. The energy provides heat and electricity to thousands of families and businesses in the area.

Biosolids can also be created from food waste. They contain important nutrients that can be added back into the soil as fertilizer. Purdue University in Indiana, for instance, has partnered with the City of West Lafayette to convert its food waste into energy and fertilizer. Meanwhile, the University of Wisconsin Oshkosh was the first in the United States to use a *dry fermentation* anaerobic digester. This process uses agricultural plant waste, the city's yard waste and wasted food from the university to power up to 10 percent of the university, which has about 13,500 students.

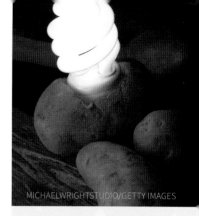

MICHAELWRIGHTSTUDIO/GETTY IMAGES

BITS + BITES

Potatoes can produce enough energy to power a clock or light bulb. That's because spuds contain starch, salt and water. When you insert two kinds of metal into the potato and add a conductor, you can generate an electrical current. Why not try your own green-energy experiment at home?

Food Waste Outside Your Home

Restaurants, grocery stores and farms are using new technologies to reduce food waste. One of the latest developments is the use of artificial intelligence (AI). It's helping more places cut back on food waste, which is better for the planet and companies' bottom lines. Here are some of the highlights:

- Farmers can use AI to figure out how to make sure their soil is healthy and to grow their crops better. Remember those dairy farmers from chapter 2? They used science and technology to improve their methods and make sure they produced enough milk to meet demand—not more.

- When food is being processed, AI helps manufacturers sort food destined for the grocery store from food that might be better used in baby food. This means ugly foods are used, not thrown away.

- Stores and restaurants use computers and data to figure out how much food they need to buy to meet their customers' needs. This ensures they don't order too many hamburgers or not enough buns. It takes the guesswork out of their businesses.

- As technology for the food industry evolves, there will be less waste—at least until the food reaches our homes. Then it's up to us to manage waste in our own kitchens.

We can reduce food waste with our families, starting with what we eat in our own kitchens.
CAVAN IMAGES/GETTY IMAGES

The ORCA machine takes food waste and turns it into water that goes down the drain.

(TOP) EVAN LORNE/SHUTTERSTOCK.COM

(MIDDLE) ORCA DIGESTERS LTD.

(BOTTOM) LITTLE ADVENTURES/SHUTTERSTOCK.COM

A Q-and-A with Louis Anagnostakos, CEO of ORCA

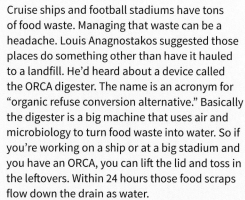

Cruise ships and football stadiums have tons of food waste. Managing that waste can be a headache. Louis Anagnostakos suggested those places do something other than have it hauled to a landfill. He'd heard about a device called the ORCA digester. The name is an acronym for "organic refuse conversion alternative." Basically the digester is a big machine that uses air and microbiology to turn food waste into water. So if you're working on a ship or at a big stadium and you have an ORCA, you can lift the lid and toss in the leftovers. Within 24 hours those food scraps flow down the drain as water.

It's a high-tech, environmentally safe, sustainable food-management system. Louis is even figuring out how to shrink the technology so we can have baby ORCAs in our homes one day. But Louis's goal isn't just to manage food scraps. It's to scrap the need for garbage trucks altogether.

Q: What got you interested in sustainable waste management?

A: I owned a company called Turtle Island Recycling based in Canada. We recycled millions of pounds of material a week. I was coming to work every day and staring at all those trucks we put on the roads. I saw a lot of food waste go into those trucks. I wanted to compost it rather than put it in a landfill. Then I started to wonder how we could deal with it without increasing our transportation footprint. I was interested in finding a no-truck solution.

Q: Where did you find the ORCA?

A: Digesters have been around since the 1970s in Korea. They were like mechanical digesters, or stomachs, that didn't require plastic bags or trucks. The technology was brought to the United States. In 2012 my company bought

it and improved it. Now software keeps track of what's being recycled and how much we're diverting. It uses existing plumbing and wastewater treatment plants to repurpose water and recapture nutrients for energy. It's not perfect, but it's significantly better than traditional collection options when it comes to protecting our planet.

Q: How much better is it?

A: The ORCA is 65 times better for the planet than sending food waste to a landfill. You're avoiding emissions created by trucking food to a landfill. And by diverting food waste from landfills, you're cutting carbon dioxide and methane gas emissions. Once at the wastewater treatment plant, the liquid can then be used to create renewable, sustainable energy. What's left over can be used for fertilizer.

Q: What do you think the future of food waste looks like?

A: Today one in every seven trucks on the road is a garbage truck. In 20 years I think we'll look back and ask, "What's a garbage truck?" If you think about it, 100 years ago people threw sewage out of their windows. Then underground pipes were invented to move liquid and human waste in a more sanitary way. The same thing will happen to waste. People will have machines to process garbage. We won't have several different trucks coming to collect garbage, recycling and food. We'll be able to do it all ourselves at home.

Q: How can kids get involved in the solution?

A: Use everything in your fridge and eat imperfect foods. We need to avoid food waste in the first place.

Composting is a great way to turn food waste into nutritious soil that can be used to grow flowers and more food.
(TOP) NATTRASS/GETTY IMAGES
(BOTTOM) EVAN LORNE/SHUTTERSTOCK.COM

Composting

It's probably hard for you to turn food scraps into safe slop for animals. It's also unlikely you can convert food waste into energy. But you can compost. Composting is a smart way to use food scraps that can't be eaten by people or animals. That's because it turns food and yard waste into nutrient-rich soil that can be returned to the earth.

Composting stops food from ending up in landfills and reduces greenhouse gas emissions. Food can be turned into fertilizer on a large scale. The strategy makes a lot of sense. For companies or cities with a lot of food waste, composting helps the planet and also saves companies money by reducing how much they truck to the landfill. This is how places like schools, stadiums and casinos are "closing the loop" on their food-recovery efforts. I "unearthed" a few great examples, which are listed on the next page.

Rising Star Elementary School in Kansas was one of the first schools to have sustainability initiatives at its school cafeteria. It banned styrofoam in 2008 and plastic straws in 2017. Cutlery is reusable, not disposable. When it comes to food, students take only what they can eat. Then they put their waste in the proper bins. Over the last few years, compost from the school cafeteria has been used in the school garden to grow more food. From 2017 to 2018 alone, Rising Star Elementary increased the amount of food it composted from 13,875 pounds (6,300 kilograms) to 27,000 pounds (12,250 kilograms). Talk about rising stars!

Ramona High School's Eco-Leaders work with the County of San Diego and the entire school district to reduce and compost food waste. In addition to tracking and measuring food waste, they donate extra food to a food pantry. Vegetable peels and leftovers from the salad bar help feed animals. And they have an Earth Tub for food that can't be fed to humans or animals. The compost is used in the high school's garden. Students learn to garden and cook, and everything they produce feeds students, their families and the community. The school's Eco-Leaders were the first high school students in California to participate in the EPA's Food Recovery Challenge.

The people at **Food for Life**, a food-recovery organization in Halton, Ontario, were frustrated with the amount of food spoiling and going to the landfill. The group was thrilled when it received a grant to buy an industrial-sized composter. The first charity in Canada to buy one, the group began transforming food waste into fertilizer—thanks to the help of some earthworms! The charity found a new way to use an old-fashioned method to reduce waste and save money. Food for Life was even named a semifinalist in the Canada Food Waste Reduction Challenge.

The **Seattle Mariners** ballpark hit a home run recently. Thanks to its food-waste initiatives, 96 percent of its food waste was diverted from the landfill. With more than two million visitors a year, that adds up to a lot of wasted food. Instead of trucking it all to the landfill, the ballpark donates thousands of pounds of extra food to food banks in Seattle. In addition, a composting program turns hundreds of pounds of food waste into soil that can be used to grow produce in the ballpark's urban garden. Food from the garden is then used in menus at the park.

San Francisco takes its food waste seriously. Other cities can learn a lot from its example.

LARRY STRONG, COURTESY OF RECOLOGY

Common Ground:
Spotlight on San Francisco

Congratulations to San Francisco—the city that composts the most in North America. In 2009 it became the first city in the United States to make composting food waste mandatory. Now it diverts about 80 percent of its waste from landfills. Compare that to New York (21 percent) and Chicago (10 percent). Huge composting facilities blend food and yard waste and sell finished soil to vineyards in wine country and nut growers in California's Central Valley. Way to go, San Fran!

Create Rich Soil at Home

Composting isn't just for cities, stadiums and schools. You can do it in your own backyard. If you add the right ingredients to the mix, your compost bin will smell earthy—not stinky—and you can use the rich compost soil in your garden.

Worms might be gross to some people, but they're heroes when it comes to turning compost into soil!
NOVAKOVAV/SHUTTERSTOCK.COM

Ingredients

- One part soil
- Two parts leaves, grass, woody materials
- One part kitchen waste, like apple cores, carrot peels, your dad's used tea bags, your grandma's coffee grounds, shredded newspapers and even dead houseplants

Directions

- Using a box made of wooden pallets, start with a layer of soil.
- Add the leaves, grass and woody materials.
- Then add kitchen waste on top.
- Water and mix your compost heap once a week and it will begin to decompose nicely. Soon you'll have beautiful soil you can reuse in your garden.

Notes

- Avoid dairy products, meat, fats and oils or you could attract pests like mice and bugs. Ew!

Soon you'll have beautiful soil that you can reuse. Everyone has a "green thumb." In the next chapter, you'll find out how much more you can do at home.

Food for Thought:
Fertilizer Facts

- Worms can speed up the process of waste turning into compost, decreasing the amount of time it takes by as much as 50 percent. It might sound gross, but using them works!

- During the composting process, temperatures in the compost pile can get as high as 100 to 150 degrees Fahrenheit (38 to 66 degrees Celsius). If you water and churn the pile regularly, you could have soil within two to three weeks instead of months.

- The color green is soothing. Even gardening or watering indoor plants has a calming effect. Some studies have shown that greenery can help our bodies heal faster from sickness or injury. Why not compost food waste so you can grow soothing indoor and outdoor plants?

- International Compost Awareness Week began in Canada in 1995. It's now celebrated around the world.

Layer and churn your compost pile, and you'll get healthy soil within weeks.

Composting Basics

KEEP OUT!
× Cooked food
× Bones
× Meat or fish
× Fats
× Grease
× Dairy
× Glass
× Aluminum
× Plastic
× Animal waste (non-herbivores)

Brown Stuff
✓ Leaves
✓ Dirt
✓ Cardboard
✓ Paper bags
✓ Wood ash
✓ Newspaper
✓ Straw
✓ Eggshells

Green Stuff
✓ Fruits
✓ Vegetables
✓ Grass
✓ Teabags
✓ Coffee grounds
✓ Plants
✓ Animal waste (herbivores)

Water the compost as needed to speed things up

Aim for a **3:1** ratio between brown material and green material.

Turn the compost to add air and regulate temperature

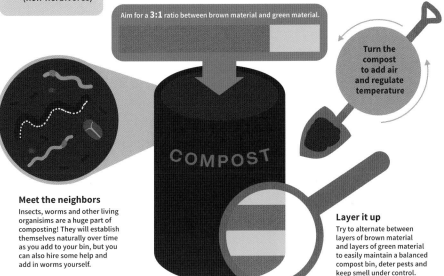

Meet the neighbors
Insects, worms and other living organisims are a huge part of composting! They will establish themselves naturally over time as you add to your bin, but you can also hire some help and add in worms yourself.

Layer it up
Try to alternate between layers of brown material and layers of green material to easily maintain a balanced compost bin, deter pests and keep smell under control.

CHOOSING A BIN

Stationary bin or pile
The classic compost pile can be easily made in your backyard. Wire, wood and even garbage cans can be used for this approach. This style will require manual turning every once in a while to aerate the compost.

Good for: Backyard composting with a simple set-up process

Tumbling bin
Rotating or tumbling bins make it easier to turn the compost by allowing you to roll or crank a handle to turn it.

Good for: Producing compost quickly (in as few as five weeks), low-effort turning of the compost, and resisting pests

Worm bin
This bin, which is also called a *vermicomposting* bin, allows for year-round composting indoors. Build your own bin, add worms and start composting! Keep the waste covered with lots of shredded paper to deter fruit flies and to limit unwanted smells.

Good for: Composting in apartments or classroms without yard space

Five

Taking a Bite out of Food Waste at Home

Of the food waste we throw away:

71%
was edible

GINO SANTA MARIA/SHUTTERSTOCK.COM

Can you guess which foods are most likely to end up in your green bin at home? Vitamin-packed fruits and vegetables. They make up over 40 percent of what we let go to waste. But the good news is, with a few easy changes you can help your family "take a bite" out of food waste.

First Things First—How Much Food Are You Wasting

Elaine Blatt works at the Oregon Department of Environmental Quality. As a food-waste scientist, she was given an important job—to investigate the amount, types and causes of wasted edible food in Oregon. Her team of researchers collected lots of data—and literally picked through compost bins—and found that 71 percent of food

FORYOU3/SHUTTERSTOCK.COM

SAVVAPANF PHOTO/SHUTTERSTOCK.COM

29%
was inedible

GOIR/SHUTTERSTOCK.COM

thrown away by families could have been eaten at one point. (Some foods, such as shells and pits, are inedible and can't be used.) Elaine has some tips for how you can do a one-week food-waste study at home:

Keep a kitchen scale and weigh how much you're putting into your compost bin.

Estimate how much was wasted. Did 1 apple go to waste or 10?

Use a diary. Look at what food was wasted. Note why it was wasted. Once you start to see how much food you're wasting, you'll pay more attention to it.

Track your food waste for a week, then add it up. Sit down with your parents and show them what you discovered. Talk about how you can reduce food waste together.

Easy Ways to Reduce Food Waste

People around the world are learning how to fight food waste at home. Here are some little things you can do to make a big difference:

Shop smarter. Think about what you want to eat in the week ahead. Go with your parents or guardians to the store. Shop only for what you need. Look in the pantry before you shop and use ingredients you already have.

Get cooking. Look for recipes you want to make with your family. You can use new or familiar ingredients. You may even have most of them in your fridge or pantry already. Some foods are traditional—or you can start new traditions. Cooking with your family is a great way to remember the value of food.

Making a list before you go to the store will help ensure that you buy only what you need so less goes to waste at home.
COURTNEY HALE/GETTY IMAGES

Use leftovers. Want leftover spaghetti for breakfast? Why not? Who says you have to eat cereal? In many cultures, the first meal of the day can include foods like rice, salad or whatever was eaten at dinner the night before. You can also use leftovers in new meals. Roast chicken can be turned into chicken salad. Extra rice can be used in a stir fry. And cooked veggies can be thrown into a frittata.

Food for Thought:
Use Your Foods

A lot of our foods go to waste because we don't know how to use them up. You probably didn't know that the crusts on your bread can be used to make croutons, bread crumbs and even French toast. Canned beans can be used in brownies (surprising but true!), and you can freeze ground meat and tomato paste to use later in dishes like chili.

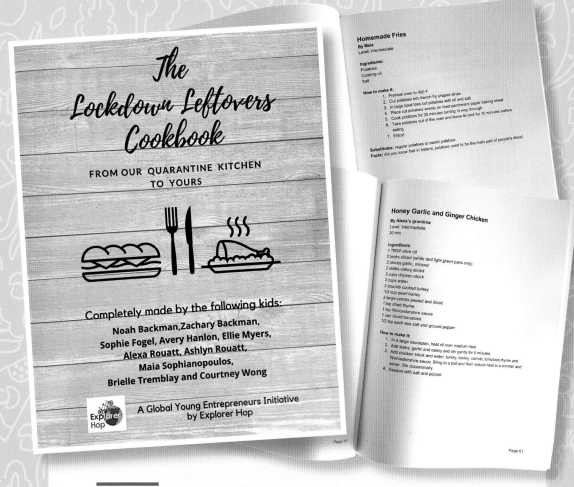

Food for Thought:

Recipe for Success

Even young kids can make a big difference in the world when they work together.

COURTESY OF SHANA FAUST

During the COVID-19 pandemic, a group of 9-to-12-year-old philanthropists from Ontario and New York City got together online to raise money to feed hungry animals at the Toronto Zoo. They decided to create, publish and sell a leftovers cookbook to give people new ways to use up foods they already had in their homes. This would help people reduce food waste, save money and not risk their health by going to the grocery store when they already had food. Called *The Lockdown Leftovers Cookbook: From Our Quarantine Kitchen to Yours*, the book has dozens of recipes that can be made from whatever leftovers people have in their fridge. "If you have chicken, you can turn it into chicken soup," says group member Sophie Fogel. "If you have leftover fruit or vegetables, you can make it into a smoothie or smoothie bowl. It tastes completely different, but you aren't wasting anything."

Ellie Myers and Sophie Fogel were part of the group that worked together to create a book of recipes you can make with leftovers in your kitchen. They donated the proceeds to a good cause.

PHOTO COURTESY OF SHANA FAUST

Rice for breakfast? Why not! It's one of Dr. Tammara Soma's favorite foods.

FOOD-WASTE HERO:

The Researcher Who Wrote the Book on Food Waste

Dr. Tammara Soma grew up in Indonesia. At mealtimes her parents often said, "Eat every single grain of rice. If you don't eat it, the rice will cry."

She says that comes from the idea that we shouldn't waste food, because it was made thanks to the sweat and tears of the farmers. "When I came to Canada, I had that in my mind," says Tammara. "It fueled me to understand the issue of food waste and how we can solve it."

Since then this food-waste expert has made big progress. In fact, she helped write a guide on how to avoid wasting food. While it's a tough problem to solve, she believes connecting people to food is key. "That one grain of rice is more than just rice," she says. "There's the farmer's hard work, the water that went into it, the animals that helped…"

Unfortunately, in many cultures food is treated as something that's okay to throw away—and that's not okay. Today it's even happening in places like Indonesia. Tammara says that instead of buying the fresh food we need, eating it and then going to the store for more, we are stocking up, stuffing it into our cars and shoving it into our fridges. That kind of pattern makes it easier to waste food.

While there aren't big "stop food waste" campaigns in Indonesia yet, Tammara likes a custom called Jumat Berkah, or Friday Blessings—a day in Muslim society to pray and give food to the needy so nothing is wasted. In her culture there's also no such thing as breakfast, lunch or dinner food. "When we have extra food, it can be eaten at any meal," she says. "We don't have toast and egg for breakfast, a sandwich for lunch and so on. In my culture, whatever I ate for dinner I can have for breakfast."

Tammara is also creative in the kitchen. She likes transforming leftovers into new dishes. Her daughter's favorite food is fried rice. "We are big rice eaters because of my background," she says. "It means that any extra rice we have, I make into fried rice, chicken porridge or chicken soup with rice." And, of course, she teaches her family that the rice will cry if they don't finish it!

Rice is a staple in many cultures. It takes hard work to collect rice, so be sure not to waste it.
FENDI ANGGORO/SHUTTERSTOCK.COM

Store better

We tend to stuff food into our fridges without thinking about where it goes as long as the door can close! But your fridge has different shelves and drawers for a reason. Put older foods in the front where you can see them. Foods like cheese, meat and vegetables should go in their crisper drawers where the temperature and humidity level is just right. Since apples ripen 6 to 10 times faster when you leave them in the fruit basket on the kitchen counter, put them in the fridge so they last longer. You can also make vegetables like carrots and celery last longer by washing them, cutting them up and putting them in water. You can even use mason jars to pickle foods like cucumbers and onions to enjoy later.

Food for Thought:
Organize Your Fridge

A recent survey by HelloFresh found that 94 percent of Australians pack their fridges wrong. Organizing the fridge by ingredients rather than by full meals can cost families up to $4,000 a year in wasted food. Professional organizer Gemma Quinn suggests organizing the fridge by grouping together foods you would use in a meal. "You'll see breakfast, lunch, dinner and snacks staring right at you." The best advice is to find a system that works best for you and your family.

Organizing your fridge so you can see all the foods you need to eat first is a great way to cut down on waste.

MARC DUFRESNE/GETTY IMAGES

Where to Store Food in Your Fridge

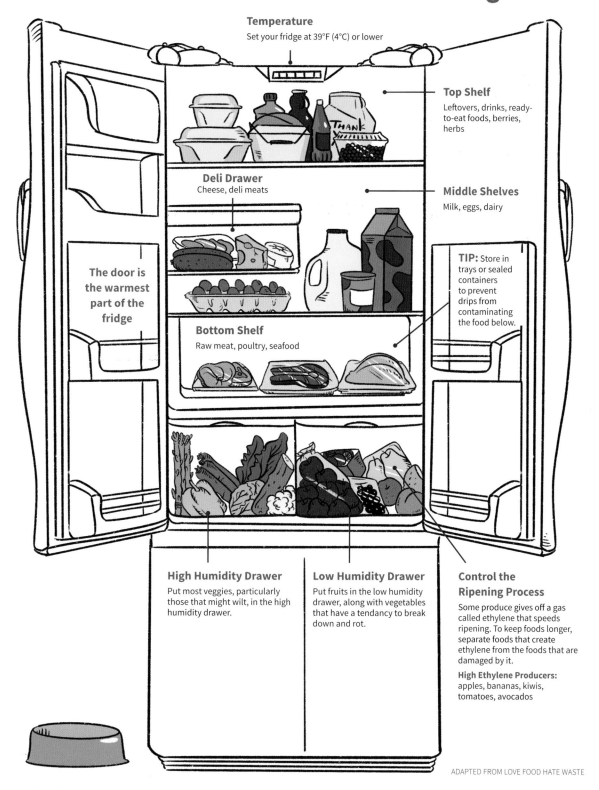

Temperature
Set your fridge at 39°F (4°C) or lower

Top Shelf
Leftovers, drinks, ready-to-eat foods, berries, herbs

Deli Drawer
Cheese, deli meats

Middle Shelves
Milk, eggs, dairy

The door is the warmest part of the fridge

TIP: Store in trays or sealed containers to prevent drips from contaminating the food below.

Bottom Shelf
Raw meat, poultry, seafood

High Humidity Drawer
Put most veggies, particularly those that might wilt, in the high humidity drawer.

Low Humidity Drawer
Put fruits in the low humidity drawer, along with vegetables that have a tendancy to break down and rot.

Control the Ripening Process
Some produce gives off a gas called ethylene that speeds ripening. To keep foods longer, separate foods that create ethylene from the foods that are damaged by it.

High Ethylene Producers: apples, bananas, kiwis, tomatoes, avocados

ADAPTED FROM LOVE FOOD HATE WASTE

A lot of foods freeze surprisingly well. What kind of foods are in your freezer?
QWART/GETTY IMAGES

BITS + BITES

When I was a kid, my mom made me and my siblings banana shakes. When your bananas are spotted and ripe, peel off the skin, break them into chunks and freeze them. When you want a cool, thick, refreshing treat, blend those frozen chunks with some milk and *voila*!

Tip: Divide the bananas into individual portions. Otherwise they'll freeze together like a block of ice.

Freeze more

Make ingredients last longer by putting them in the freezer. You can put nuts and almond flour in the freezer. Take them out later when you want to make gluten-free carrot muffins or breakfast cookies. You can also freeze your grapes before they spoil. They make a refreshing treat or can be used instead of ice cubes in your lemonade. Bread, milk, hummus, vegetables, tomato sauce, meat, cheese, chocolate, nuts, herbs and even eggs (without the shell) can be frozen. You can even freeze entire meals and microwave them another time.

Understand best-before dates ···················

Use your head when it comes to expiry dates. Look at foods, smell them, and use common sense to tell if something is bad. Too many people throw food out when it's past its expiry date. Instead we should use our heads, or rather our noses, to decide when our food has gone bad. The key is to use common sense and be your own judge.

Donate ··

Nonperishable and unspoiled perishable food can be donated to local food banks, soup kitchens, pantries and shelters. The young members of one hockey team in Toronto got together to donate food and funds to the Daily Bread Food Bank. It was a great way to feed people in need. Or if you have extra food at home—say, delicious homemade cookies or banana bread—why not share with a friend? In Denmark it's a tradition to give food to neighbors before leaving for vacation. It's a great way to make sure good food gets eaten—and to make friends!

Don't get rid of milk just because the best-before date has passed. Smell it first to decide whether it has gone bad. If it hasn't been opened, there's a good chance it's still okay to drink.
WATTANAPHOB/GETTY IMAGES

Check your pantry to see what ingredients you have in stock before you buy more.
HASPHOTOS/SHUTTERSTOCK.COM

How will you observe Compost Awareness Week?

RENATA ANGERAMI/GETTY IMAGES

Compost ·

We've already talked a lot about composting—and for good reason. You can put your food scraps in the green compost bin provided by your local government. Many municipalities have had programs in place since before you were born, and more are joining in. You already know how to start a compost pile in your backyard and use the fertilizer in your garden. There are lots of great books and online resources to teach you how to do this at home if you want to learn more.

Save the date ·

There are several days and weeks during the year earmarked for raising awareness about food waste.

The United Nations named September 29 **International Day of Awareness of Food Loss and Waste**.

World Food Day, a day for supporting food security and fighting hunger, is on October 16.

Earth Week leads up to **Earth Day** on April 22.

Stop Food Waste Day is on the last Wednesday of April during Earth Month.

Food Waste Action Week (UK) is in March.

Waste Reduction Week in Canada is in October. Pay special attention to **Food Waste Friday**.

Canadian national **Clean Out Your Fridge Day** is in November. Use up your ingredients before they go bad!

International Compost Awareness Week is in May. There's also **National Learn About Composting Day (US)** at the end of that month.

Ask your parents or teacher if you can attend events like the **Zero Waste Conference**, even online.

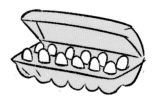

Good News! Food-Waste Action Campaigns Are Working

An organization called Love Food Hate Waste (which runs campaigns all over the world) polled Canadians partway through the COVID-19 pandemic to find out whether their food-waste habits had changed during the crisis. Results showed that more people were better at shopping smarter, freezing food and using food they already had at home. This is probably because people didn't want to waste money or risk their health going to the store to buy food they didn't need during a pandemic. In fact:

24 percent of households said they were throwing away or composting less uneaten food.

94 percent were motivated to reduce their household's avoidable food waste.

LoveFoodHateWaste.com is a great site with lots of ideas and information to inspire people all over the world to reduce food waste.

We started to shop smarter and waste less during the pandemic. Now let's keep it up!

WESTEND61/GETTY IMAGES

There are lots of cool ways to make ingredients last longer, like keeping green onions in water.

MEHRIBAN ALIYEVA/GETTY IMAGES

Start a Food-Waste Campaign at School

Now that you know so much about food waste, you can teach others. Why not help your school with a food-waste action plan? A few ideas can help you get started:

☐ Involve your school and cafeteria staff in a food-waste audit. How much are you wasting and why?

☐ Make posters about how reducing food waste helps the planet. Put them up in classrooms and in the cafeteria.

☐ Remind kids to take or bring only the food they can eat.

☐ Some schools have share tables where students can put unopened food like milk cartons, packaged foods and whole fruit. These items can be eaten by others.

☐ Ask cafeteria staff to *offer* food, rather than *serve* it so kids don't feel like they have to take food they won't eat. A single word change can make a difference.

☐ Put healthy foods within reach so kids can grab them easily in the lunch line. It's also a good idea to cut them into slices so kids can have part of an apple or orange instead of a whole one.

☐ Make lunch longer. One study showed that by making lunch 30 minutes instead of 20, food waste can be reduced by nearly one-third.

☐ Schedule recess before lunch. After playing outside, kids come to lunch hungry. This can reduce food waste and increase the amount of healthy foods they eat.

☐ Start a compost program. If students put food scraps in a separate bin, those scraps can be composted and used as plant fertilizer.

☐ Let your teachers know there are lots of resources online to help them learn more.

Share your food-waste knowledge at school. Challenge your school to reduce food waste and see how well you can do.
TOP: L-L HELTON, COLQUITZ MIDDLE SCHOOL
BOTTOM: MASKOT/GETTY IMAGES

Why waste unopened food when someone else can eat it? Ask if your school can start a sharing box or table.
KING COUNTRY GREEN SCHOOLS PROGRAM

This is my pantry at home. These foods are on a low shelf so my kids can help pack their own lunches and take what they will eat.

ERIN SILVER

Get involved in packing your own lunch for school. When you work hard to make something, you're less likely to waste it.

VGAJIC/GETTY IMAGES

Small Changes Can Make a Big Difference

Administrators at the University of California, Santa Barbara took matters into their own hands. Or rather they took matters out of students' hands. In 2009 the director of dining services realized that those plastic rectangular cafeteria trays led students to load their trays with as much food as they could carry. A lot of it went to waste. The director wanted to see what would happen if the dining hall stopped using trays and gave students plates instead. Something did change: the amount of food waste per person decreased by 50 percent. That's 5,000 pounds (2,300 kilograms) of wasted food a day, cut in half.

After this "taste" of success, the university made another change. Rather than let students pile food onto their plates, cafeteria staff pre-portioned it. Students got the amount of food they *should* be eating rather than what they thought they *could* eat. Big portions encourage people to overeat and can lead to a lot of waste. The university's experiments showed that little changes can have a big impact.

Taking away food trays and pre-portioning meals help reduce the amount of food students waste.

MASKOT/GETTY IMAGES

BITS + BITES

Kehkashan Basu was born in Dubai and studied in Canada. She founded Green Hope to empower people in poor countries to fight the climate crisis by planting trees. She also reduces hunger by teaching people to grow foods like beans and spinach. At age 12 she spoke at the United Nations and quoted Gandhi. "You must be the change you wish to see in the world," she said. Kehkashan hopes other kids will be inspired by her work and her words.

Kids can bring about change. There are so many inspiring stories. Maybe yours can be one of them.

RANGEECHA/SHUTTERSTOCK.COM

My Food-Waste Journey Continues

I had a hunch my family was wasting too much food, but how much were we wasting and why? And what could we do about it? My kids helped me find some answers. On the first week of our study, we filled our green bin with compost as usual. Before taking it to the curb, we put it on a scale to see how much it weighed. After the compost had been collected, we stood it on the scale again. That week we had wasted about 20 pounds (9 kilograms) of food. "That's disgusting!" one of my kids said.

We knew we could do better. But we quickly realized that the more fruits and veggies we ate, the more the compost would weigh. Watermelon peels are heavy! We used tips from chapter 5 to see if we could improve. Over the next few weeks, we did. Instead of throwing out overripe bananas, we made banana bread and those same banana shakes my mom used to make for me. With leftover edamame, I popped the beans out of the shells and used them in shepherd's pie. When we couldn't finish a roast chicken, we fed some meat

My son, Josh, helped me measure our food waste at home. Then we brainstormed ways to cut back on how much we waste.

ERIN SILVER

to our puppy, Piper, and froze the bones for chicken soup. Of course, this soup calls for carrots. Instead of throwing the green tops in the compost, I used them in a recipe for pesto sauce, which was delicious on the pasta I found in the pantry.

After a few weeks we had reduced our waste by a lot. We are still making good decisions to curb how much we waste. My family also volunteers to make sandwiches for homeless people in our city through a local humanitarian organization. It makes us feel good to do what we can to help the planet and fight food insecurity. And we're still finding new ways to cut back on food waste even more. I know you can too.

Yummy! Who doesn't love fresh banana bread right from the oven? Old bananas make banana bread even sweeter.
VGAJIC/GETTY IMAGES

Glossary

anaerobic digestion—the process through which biodegradable waste, such as food scraps, leaves and yard waste, is turned into renewable energy

biodigester—a device that breaks down natural waste products like manure or food, either anaerobically (without oxygen) or aerobically (with oxygen)

biogas—a fuel created by the decomposition of organic matter, such as food, manure and plants

biosolids—organic materials created from treating wastewater and used to improve soil as fertilizer

carbon dioxide—a colorless, odorless gas made of carbon and oxygen atoms. It's a greenhouse gas that traps heat in the atmosphere and contributes to global warming.

carbon footprint—the amount of carbon dioxide released into the air by the activities of a person, company or country in a given period

composting—converting natural products like food scraps or leaves into a rich fertilizer through decomposition

dry fermentation—the process of breaking down natural products like food and solid waste (garbage) without adding liquid or manure to help

food insecurity—the state of being unable to consistently access or afford enough food

food justice—the view that access to nutritious, affordable, culturally appropriate food is a human right

food recovery/food rescue—the practice of preventing food from being thrown in the garbage

food waste—all the food that is thrown away, either edible (food that wasn't eaten on time and spoiled, or someone chose not to eat it) or inedible (what you can't eat, like peach pits, banana peels and eggshells)

gigaton—a unit of measurement that equals one billion metric tons

gleaning—collecting leftover crops from farmers' fields after the crop has been harvested or from fruit trees in residential areas when the fruit has fallen on public property

greenhouse gas emissions—discharges of gases such as carbon dioxide, methane and nitrous oxide, released into the air in huge quantities usually as a result of human activities, which then trap heat, warm the planet and contribute to the climate crisis

groundwater contamination—the tainting of the water within the earth, caused by human-made products like fertilizer, pesticides, gasoline, oil, road salts or other chemicals leaching into the ground. This makes the wells and springs the groundwater feeds into unsafe for people.

landfills—places where garbage is taken after people throw it away; often called dumps

locavores—people who make an effort to eat food that is grown, raised or produced by suppliers nearby, usually within 100 miles (160 kilometers) of where they live

methane—a colorless, odorless, flammable greenhouse gas that is contributing to global warming. Sources include natural gas, volcanoes and even the gas released from cows.

plant-based foods—foods that don't have animal products or artificial ingredients in them, mainly made from fruits, nuts, beans, seeds and grains

ration—use sparingly (sometimes people have to ration food)

renewable energy—energy that comes from natural sources like the sun, wind and waves and can be replenished

seasonal foods—foods that are available, plentiful and ripe during a particular season of the year

shelf-stable foods—items that can be stored on shelves or in the pantry for a long time without spoiling, such as canned goods, rice, fruit juice and mustard

silvopastoral farming—a kind of farming that integrates trees, plants and livestock on the same land, thereby creating healthier soils, fewer greenhouse gas emissions and more robust cattle

supply-chain management—the supervision of the people and activities involved in producing products or materials, from beginning to end

sustainable food management—a systematic approach to reducing food waste and its impacts on all the resources involved, from growing food to disposing of it

ugly food—produce that's considered too ripe, green, big, small or misshapen to be sold at grocery stores

United Nations (UN)—an international organization created to promote international peace, security and cooperation; headquartered in New York, it currently has 193 members

vegan—someone who doesn't eat any meat or animal products, including poultry, fish, seafood, dairy and eggs

vegetarians—people who don't eat meat, poultry, fish or seafood

Resources

Print

Andrus, Aubre. *101 Small Ways to Change the World.* Lonely Planet Global Limited, 2018.

Appelhof, Mary, and Joanne Olszewski. *Worms Eat My Garbage, 35th Anniversary Edition: How to Set Up and Maintain a Worm Composting System; Compost Food Waste, Produce Fertilizer for Houseplants and Garden, and Educate Your Kids and Family.* Storey Publishing, LLC, 2017.

Brisson, Pat. *Before We Eat: From Farm to Table.* Tilbury House Publishers, 2018.

Brown, Renata. *Gardening Lab for Kids: 52 Fun Experiments to Learn, Grow, Harvest, Make, Play, and Enjoy Your Garden.* Quarry Books, 2014.

Carlson, Laurie. *Green Thumbs: A Kid's Activity Guide to Indoor and Outdoor Gardening.* Chicago Review Press, 2012.

Clinton, Chelsea. *It's Your World: Get Informed, Get Inspired & Get Going!* Penguin Young Readers Group, 2015.

DiOrio, Rana. *What Does It Mean to Be Green?* Sourcebooks, 2010.

Donnelly, Rebecca. *Green Machine: The Slightly Gross Truth about Turning Your Food Scraps into Green Energy.* Henry Holt and Co., 2020.

Heinecke, Liz Lee. *Outdoor Science Lab for Kids: 52 Family-Friendly Experiments for the Yard, Garden, Playground, and Park.* Quarry Books, 2016.

Idzikowski, Lisa. *Ecology in Your Everyday Life: Real World Science.* Enslow Publishing, LLC, 2019.

Ignotofsky, Rachel. *The Wondrous Workings of Planet Earth: Understanding Our World and Its Ecosystems.* Clarkson Potter/Ten Speed, 2018.

Mangor, Jodie. *Climate Change and Food Production: Taking Earth's Temperature.* Britannica Digital Learning, 2019.

Reilly, Kathleen M. *Food: 25 Amazing Projects Investigate the History and Science of What We Eat.* Nomad Press, 2010.

Seaver, Barton. *National Geographic Kids Cookbook: A Year-Round Fun Food Adventure.* Disney Book Group, 2014.

Veness, Kimberley. *Let's Eat: Sustainable Food for a Hungry Planet.* Orca Book Publishers, 2017.

World Book. *Food, Water, and Climate Change.* World Book, Inc., 2019.

Videos

Americans Waste Up to 40 Percent of the Food They Produce. PBS NewsHour, 2019.

Canadians Get Creative in Solving Food Waste Problem. CBC News: The National, 2018.

Food Waste Causes Climate Change. Here's How We Stop It. Our Changing Climate, 2020.

Food Waste: How Much Food Do Supermarkets Throw Away? CBC Marketplace, 2016.

Food Waste Is the World's Dumbest Problem. Vox, 2017.

Food Waste: Last Week Tonight with John Oliver. HBO, 2015.

Food-Waste Rebel Wants You to Eat Ugly Food. National Geographic, 2014.

How Denver Is Tackling Food Waste to Fight Hunger, Climate Change. PBS NewsHour, 2020.

How Rotting Vegetables Make Electricity/World Wide Waste. Business Insider, 2021.

How This Urban Farm Creates 300,000 lbs of Compost by Hand. Our Changing Climate, 2020.

Is France's Groundbreaking Food-Waste Law Working? PBS NewsHour, 2019.

Just Eat It: A Food Waste Story. foodwastemovie.com, 2014.

Kids Go Green: Reducing Food Waste. PBS LearningMedia, 2018.

London's Rubbish Problem: Food Waste. BBC London News, 2017.

The Diet That Helps Fight Climate Change. Vox, 2017.

Ugly Food: A Solution to Food Wastage? The Feed SBS, 2015.

Wasted! The Story of Food Waste. Amazon Prime Video, 2017.

Why Do We Waste Perfectly Good Food in the U.S.? Al Jazeera, 2018.

WWF's Food Waste Warrior School Program. worldwildlife.org, 2018.

Websites

Food Matters Action Kit: cec.org/flwy

Love Food Hate Waste Canada: lovefoodhatewaste.ca/5-ways

McKinsey for Kids: mckinsey.com/featured-insights/mckinsey-for-kids/
  food-waste-not-want-not

Save the Food: savethefood.com

Second Harvest Food Rescue: secondharvest.ca

Too Good To Go: toogoodtogo.com

University of California Climate Lab: climate.universityofcalifornia.edu

Wasted Food: wastedfood.com

Acknowledgments

The great thing about writing nonfiction books is that I get to study all angles of a subject from leading experts in different fields. This book involved a great deal of research, and I express my gratitude to the following people and organizations for their time and help with this book. Thanks to (in no particular order) Dr. Enrique Salmón (Cal State East Bay), Kay Cornelius (Panorama Meats), Lori Nikkel (Second Harvest), Jonathan Bloom (wastedfood.com), Rick Nahmias (Food Forward), Leslie Mohr and Amber Rood (Barnana), Rachel Kimel (Bowery Project), Kirsten Duggan (Sweet Acres Pig Sanctuary), Louis Anagnostakos (ORCA), Elaine Blatt (Oregon Department of Environmental Quality) and Dr. Tammara Soma (Simon Fraser University) for speaking with me.

The staff on their teams who helped coordinate interviews, fact-check statistics and provide graphics played an invaluable role. Andre Villasenor from the EPA was a huge help. I also really enjoyed reading about and watching videos from Tristram Stuart, the University of California Climate Lab, the Environmental Protection Agency, Food Matters Action Kit, ReFed and Love Food Hate Waste. So many organizations are doing an incredible job of reducing food waste at the source, feeding people who need it or working on other important solutions to a problem that affects us all. Your "hunger" for justice is inspiring.

Thanks also to my editor, Kirstie Hudson, and the whole team at Orca for listening to my ideas and giving me the chance to write books that make a difference. To my mom, thanks for visiting farmers' markets with me and teaching me about composting and food waste from a young age. Your teachings definitely stuck! And thanks as always to my boys for listening to me talk about food waste ad nauseam for the last few years. Finally, I want to acknowledge my friends and family for eating my (slightly expired) food and joining me on this journey to reduce food waste at home.

Index

*Page numbers in **bold** indicate an image caption.*

Erin Silver is a children's author and freelance writer whose work has appeared in everything from *Good Housekeeping* to the *Washington Post*. She is the author of numerous books for children, including *Rush Hour: Navigating Our Global Traffic Jam* in the Orca Footprints line, as well as *What Kids Did: Stories of Kindness and Invention in the Time of COVID-19* and *Proud to Play: Canadian LGBTQ+ Athletes Who Made History*. Erin holds a master of fine arts in creative nonfiction from the University of King's College in Halifax, Nova Scotia, a postgraduate journalism degree from Toronto Metropolitan University and a bachelor of arts from the University of Toronto.

Suharu Ogawa is a Toronto-based illustrator. Her love for drawing started in a kindergarten art school after being kicked out of calligraphy class for refusing to convert to right-handedness. Formally trained in art history and cultural anthropology, she worked for several years as a university librarian until her passion for illustration called her out of that career and into the pursuit of a lifelong dream. Since then, Suharu has created illustrations for magazines, public art projects and children's books, including *Why Humans Work: How Jobs Shape Our Lives and Our World* in the Orca Think line. She also teaches illustration at OCAD University in Toronto.

THE MORE YOU KNOW
THE MORE YOU GROW

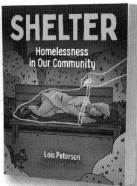
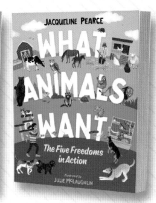
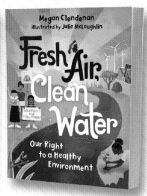

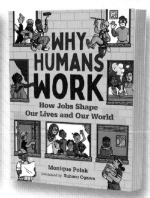

WHAT'S THE BIG IDEA?

The **Orca Think** series introduces us to the issues making headlines in the world today. It encourages us to question, connect and take action for a better future. With those tools we can all become better citizens. Now that's smart thinking!